My Invisible Daddy

A Children's Book About God and His Love for Them

Valerie C. Muñoz

Illustrated by Touba Nateghi

Higgins Publishing

DALLAS, TX

My Invisible Daddy:
A Children's Book About God and His Love for Them
Published in 2023 by Higgins Publishing * HigginsPublishing.com
Written by Valerie C. Muñoz * Copyright ©2022-2023 * All Rights Reserved

The opinions expressed by the author are not necessarily those of Higgins Publishing.

Higgins Publishing is committed to excellence in the publishing industry. The company reflects the philosophy established by the founder, based on Psalm 68:11, "The Lord gave the word and great was the company of those who published it."

~ ~ ~

Library of Congress Control Number 2023904248
Muñoz, Valerie C. * Pages cm. 28

978-1-941580-82-0 (HB) * 978-1-941580-79-0 (PB)
978-1-941580-55-4 (EPUB)

My Invisible Daddy:
A Children's Book About God and His Love for Them
Higgins Publishing 1st Edition
June 2023

SUBJECTS:
Juvenile NonFiction / Religion / Christian
Emotions & Feelings

Juvenile NonFiction / Health & Daily Living / Safety

Juvenile NonFiction / Family / Parents

For information about special discounts, fundraising, bulk purchases, subsidiary, foreign and translation rights & permissions, please contact, Higgins Publishing at contact@higginspublishing.com.

SCAN TO REVIEW

Thank You For Your Purchase!

~ ~ ~

If You Enjoy This Book
Please Post A Review
Where You Purchased This Book,
or SCAN the QR Code
To Post A Review At Amazon.

Thank You!

Matthew 19:14, "But Jesus said, Suffer little children, and forbid them not, to come unto me: for of such is the kingdom of heaven (KJV)."

To my arrows, the men in my life who will always be my boys,
Eddie Jr., Nicholas, Michael, Moses and my grandchildren,
Maliah, Jaden, Maxton!

To all the Nations and generations of children
who grew up without a physical daddy!

One Saturday morning, Valentine and her little brother, Lucky, were excited because their mommy called them after they hadn't seen her for three days. Valentine's mommy would pick them up and take them to a birthday party!

There would be cake, ice cream, games, and best of all, a Piñata.
Valentine and Lucky were alone often. Their older siblings worked.
Eight-year-old Valentine usually had to watch her little brother.
While it was sometimes hard for Valentine to take care of her five-year-old
brother, they usually had lots of fun together. They kept each other company,
inventing many games.

Valentine and Lucky got ready.
Valentine said, "Lucky, stay clean and
don't get dirty, Mommy will be here soon!
Lucky smiled and said, "OK, but when
is Mommy coming?" Valentine and Lucky
waited, and waited, and waited!
Lucky again asked,
"But when is Mommy coming?"

Valentine sighed, "Well, Mommy will be here soon but don't get dirty, OK?"
Lucky asked again, "But when is Mommy coming?"
Then Lucky went to the refrigerator and grabbed some syrup without pancakes!
He loved syrup and began sharing with his dogs,
King and Ozo. Sometimes, Lucky could be a bit of an imp (or a handful).

Valentine said, "Oh no, you gave them syrup?" King and Ozo had syrup all over their ears, nose, and tails but this did not bother them! They felt Lucky getting very sad, so they begin to chase each other and make Valentine and Lucky laugh! They all ran outside, where there was a little pond filled with water and mud. King and Ozo jumped into the pond.

And guess who followed them?
If you guessed, Lucky, you're right!
Five-year-old Lucky jumped into the muddy pond
along with his best friends, King and Ozo!

Valentine put her hands up in the air, saying,
"Lucky, you're all dirty now!" He had syrup all over
his face, his hair, and hands, and mud all over his clothes!
He was drenched in water!

Lucky put his face in his hands and begin
to cry, "When is Mommy coming,
when?" King and Ozo jumped up
at Lucky and began
licking his face.

Valentine put her chin in the palms of her hands, looking up into the sky, wondering when her mommy would come? If she would come? Did she forget again? It was now nighttime, and the moon was shining bright!

Valentine and Lucky decided to play their favorite sliding socks game! They put on lots of socks and would race from one side of their long living room wood floor to the other side! King and Ozo joined them!
Then their mommy came through the door!

Lucky jumped for joy, saying, "Mommy, Mommy, you're here?" Mommy had a box of pizza in one hand and two party bags in the other. Valentine sat on the couch, looking perplexed and sad. Mommy put Lucky on her lap. Lucky looked at the candy bags and said angrily, "Why did you not take us to the birthday party?" Once Mommy showed Lucky all the candy in the party bags, his face got happy, and he was on Mommy's lap, smiling!

Mommy sat Lucky down and gave him a slice of yummy pizza. She hugged Valentine and said, "Here, eat, Mommy will be back!" Mommy went towards the door. Lucky ran towards her saying, "No, Mommy! No, Mommy, don't go, don't go!" But Mommy began closing the door behind her, saying, "Valentine, take care of your brother! I have to go to work! I'll be back!" And just like that, she was gone again! Valentine tried to help Lucky.

Lucky cried at the top of his lungs. He yelled like an angry lion, kicked his feet on the floor, and fought with the air! Valentine tried to hold and calm him, but Lucky would not stop crying! He shouted, "I want my mommy! I want my mommy!"
This seemed like forever, but then he hugged Valentine. Valentine hugged her little brother, Lucky. Tears fell from her eyes, but she did not yell like a lion, and she did not kick her feet on the floor. Valentine did not fight with the air.
She held Lucky until he fell asleep.

Valentine then put a pillow under Lucky's head and covered her little brother with a blanket. Then she thought to herself. Mommy did not understand that Valentine and Lucky did not want candy, they did not want a pizza or even to go to a birthday party! They just wanted time with their mommy. Valentine put her face in the palms of her hands and began to cry silently. After all, she was just an eight-year-old girl.

Looking at Lucky now sound
asleep she was afraid!
She prayed, "God if you are
real, please bring my
Mommy home safe.

God please help me to be a
good mommy one day. And
please make me feel safe so
that I can sleep."

All of a sudden, Valentine felt a warm magnetic energy!
It felt like the heat from the sun shining on her face and all
over her body as if she was getting the biggest hug ever!

Valentine was no longer afraid or sad.
She felt peaceful, and just like that, she fell right to sleep.

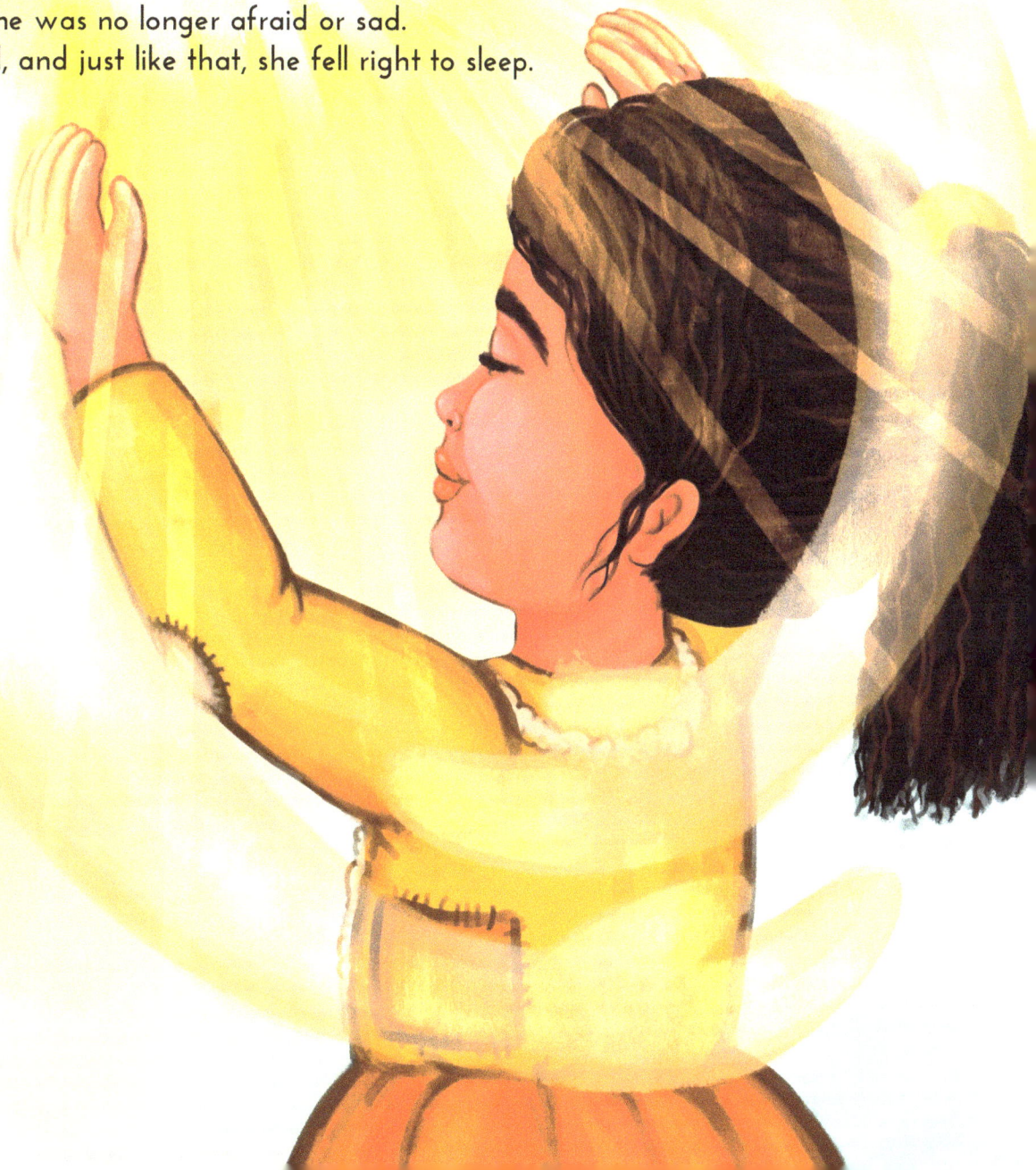

Valentine and Lucky woke up on Sunday morning. King and Ozo were waiting outside for them to play! Valentine saw the Big Yellow School Bus! This bus came every Sunday to pick up children and parents, taking them to Sunday church!

Valentine dressed herself and Lucky, and off they went to have fun! They would sing songs, learn wonderful Bible stories about Jesus, and get their bellies full of peanut butter sandwiches, bananas, and a snack. Their Sunday School teachers gave them warm smiles, making them feel safe and happy!

SCHOOL BUS

Valentine and Lucky were guided into the adult church with all the other children. There was a tall man with a scary voice, and Lucky was afraid! But Valentine, held on tightly to Lucky's hand. The tall man with the scary voice sang this song...

Jesus loves the little children, all the children of the world, red, yellow, black and white, they are precious in his sight. Jesus loves the little children of the world.
(Clare Herbert Woolston 1800)

Over and over, the tall man with the scary voice sang these words!

The tall man with the big, loud voice put his hand on Valentine's head and said these words, "But Jesus said, Leave the children alone, and do not forbid them to come to Me; for the kingdom of heaven belongs to such as these." After laying His hands on them, He departed from there. (Matthew 19:14-15, NASB)

Valentine felt the same magnetic energy and big hug she felt when she was afraid and prayed that night when her mommy left, closing the door behind them, and Lucky cried himself to sleep.

Valentine heard in her mind and thoughts,
a voice softly speaking to her while
the tall man was praying for her.
The words were, "I am your daddy!
I will always take care of you when your
mommy is not there. I will never leave
or fail you. Always trust me, even though
you don't see me. I am always near!"

That day Valentine called
God her Invisible Daddy!

The bus arrived on Adventure Street where
Valentine and Lucky lived! And guess who was
waiting for them when they jumped off the bus?
Yes! Did you guess right? King and Ozo!
Oh, and their mommy, too!!!

Valentine also knew that God,
her Invisible Daddy, would always be near!

"A Father to the Fatherless;
God meets the lonely in Families."
(Psalms 68:5-6 - Paraphrased)

ABOUT THE AUTHOR

Valerie C. Muñoz has a Master's Degree in Marriage and Family Therapy and a Bachelor's of Science in Child Development. Currently she is pursuing her Ph.D. in Depth Psychology, specializing in Integrative Therapy and Healing practices. Valerie became pregnant at seventeen and began her family, resulting in four children and three grandchildren. She began her journey servicing at-risk communities through entrepreneurship and establishing a family day care home for over twenty-five years. Valerie was inspired the moment she held her first son in her arms as a teenage mother and this became the motivation for understanding child development.

Over time, she has collaborated with many non-profit organizations, such as Options Food Program, the International Institute of Los Angeles, Mexican American Opportunity Foundation and the Department of Children and Family Services. Valerie's gift of working with traumatized children from childhood motivated her to attend East Los Angeles College, where her journey to higher education began. Her experiences provided a means for her to raise her children and discover the vast need for mental health services. As a Family Day Care Provider Valerie observed the many challenges with single mother's and at-risk families that often resulted in open DCFS cases and children placed into foster care.

Valerie has worked as a marriage and family therapist for over seven years in organizations such as Aviva and Family Services, Hathaway-Sycamores, Single Parent's of Power, and El Nido Family Centers. Moreover, she has been an advocate for children and families, interventionist, educator, youth mentor and inspirational coach.

SCAN TO BUY

Please Spread The Love & Gift Copies
To Foster Children, Latchkey Kids &
Adopted or Fatherless Children.

Thank You!

www.ingramcontent.com/pod-product-compliance
Lightning Source LLC
Chambersburg PA
CBHW042344030426
42335CB00030B/3457